CW01218348

Poems for People

Fiona Hamilton

TWO TURTLES
PRESS

www.twoturtlespress.com

POEMS FOR PEOPLE

© Two Turtles Press

© Fiona Hamilton Text & Illustrations 2005

First published in the United Kingdom in 2005 by
Two Turtles Press
PO Box 2561, Bristol BS6 9BB

www.twoturtlespress.com

Design by Fiona Hamilton
Illustrations by Fiona Hamilton,
Joe Bailward, Anna Bailward and Olivia Bailward

Printed by Doveton Press Ltd, Bristol 0117 966 0078

ISBN 0-9551654-0-7
978-0-9551654-0-5
British Library Cataloguing in Publication Data available

All rights reserved.
No part of this publication may be reproduced,
stored in a retrieval system, or transmitted, in any form
or by any means, electronic, mechanical,
photocopying, recording or otherwise,
without prior permission of the publishers.

For Tom,
Joe, Anna and Olivia
with love

Acknowledgements are due to the editors
of the following publications, in which
some of these poems have appeared:
*Poetry Life, Bristol Evening Post,
Poem on a Postcard, North Words,
'Goldilocks Says Sorry' –
winner of the Belmont Poetry Prize 2005*

Thanks to

Co-authors of 'Silver Man'
Melanie Bennette and Anna Bailward

Colin Brown, Director, Poetry Can

Special thanks to Joe, Anna and Olivia for their pictures

United Bristol Healthcare **NHS**
NHS Trust
Bristol Royal Hospital for Children Arts Programme

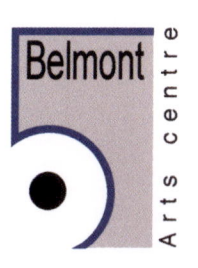

POEMS FOR PEOPLE

Things I Like	1
Reflection	3
Fascinating Facts	4
Footprints	6
Secrets	8
SATs	9
Trees	11
Proud Cat	12
Seal	14
Cricket	16
Allergic to Spinach	17
Questions	18
Goldilocks Says Sorry	19
Ice Cream	21
Pen y Fan	23
Animal Antics	24
Valentine's Message	26
Summer	28
Beach	29
Silver Man	30
Egyptian Kaleidoscope	33
Skating	35
Celebration	36
A Poet's Wish	37

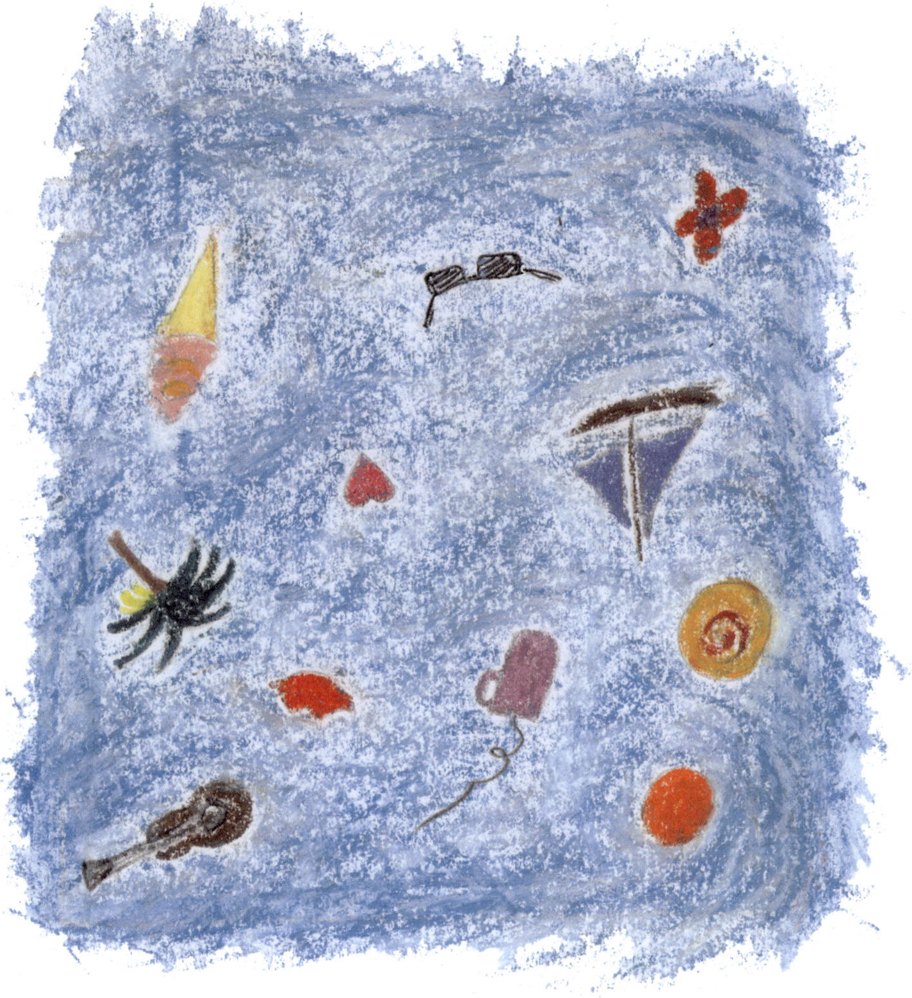

Things I like

I like my crisps crisp
My honey runny
My oranges sweet
My jokes funny

I like my cornflakes flakey
My ice creams cold
My doughnuts jammy
My hearts gold

I like my lemonade fizzy
My coffee strong
My peanut butter crunchy
My summers long

I like my eggs easy over
My jam spread thick
My bananas yellow
My poems quick

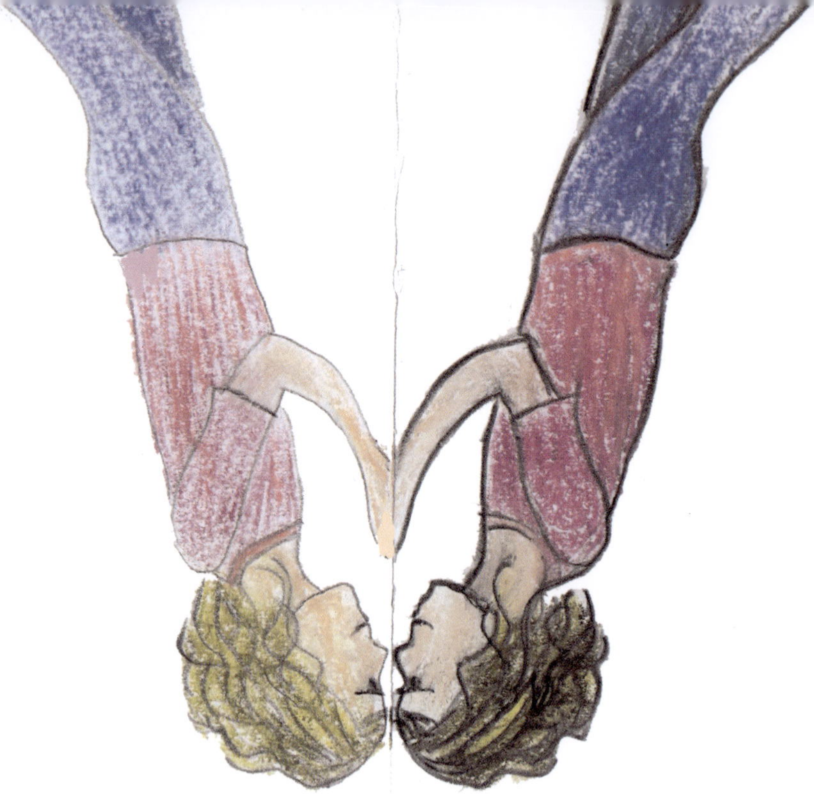

Reflection

I look in the mirror
What do I see
I see her
Looking at me

I say:
'Hey!
Hey you there!
Get a brush
And tidy up your hair'

She says:
'Hey!
Hey you there!
Excuse me
Don't just stand and stare'

She says:
'I'm very busy
I've got things to do
So first YOU get the brush
And tidy up YOU!'

Fascinating facts

The axolotl is a Mexican salamander
that never grows up

Mmm

A chameleon's tongue
is twice the length of its body

Mmmm

The Chilean frog has glands on its bum
that swell up to look like an extra pair of eyes

Mmmmm

There's such a thing as an exploding cucumber
Some tropical mushrooms glow green at night

Mmmmmm

Dragons exist
Bacteria are our distant cousins

Mmmmmmm

Barnacles use their legs to feed with
and are neither male nor female

Mmmmmmmm

The female Bonellia spoon worm is two metres long
The male Bonellia spoon worm is one millimetre long
He lives inside her body

Mmmmmmmmm

Some starfish have fifty arms

Uh-huh?

They can make banana milkshake
change channels on the TV
and strum their favourite tune on a guitar
all at once

Footprints

There are footprints on the pavement
They're leading us somewhere
They're kind of brown and muddy
Maybe it's a bear

Or maybe it's a monster
With yellow spotty shoes
Or maybe it's a dragon
Who's leaving cryptic clues

To lead us to his cavern
Deep down underground
A slippery scary cavern
That makes a gruffly sound

Maybe it's a builder
Who's building in the street
But I think it's a wuffalo
Who hasn't cleaned his feet

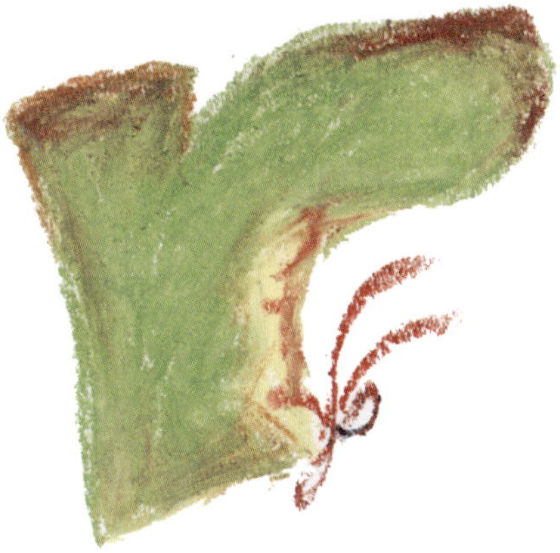

Secrets

ponies nuzzling noses
a hidden path to a dell
chocolate eggs on an egg hunt
a pale blue speckled shell

a mossy seat for a fairy
a wood where pixies go
fields of tufted grasses
a hedge where violets grow

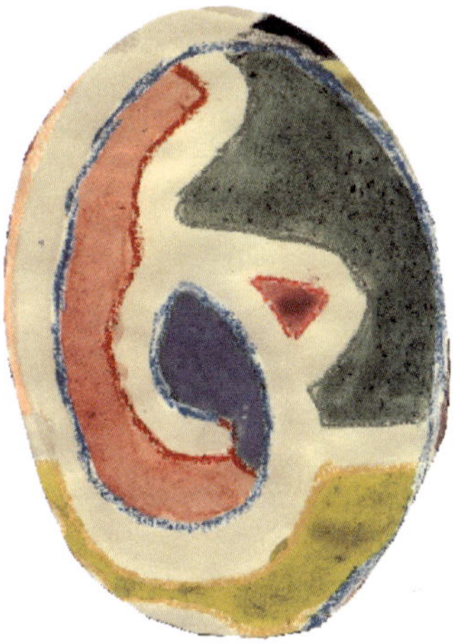

SATs

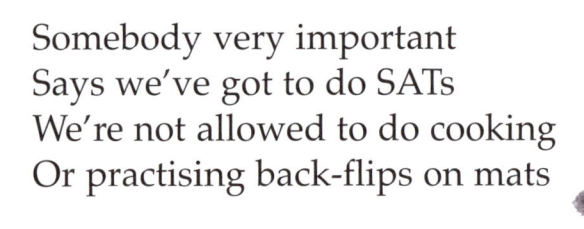

Somebody very important
Says we've got to do SATs
We're not allowed to do cooking
Or practising back-flips on mats

Or planting trees in the playground
Or looking for rivers on maps
Miss Morris says it's official
We've got to sit still and do SATs

Billy got put on the sad board
For saying the teachers were stressy
And Lucy lost four golden minutes
For making her adding all messy

Mum says they're giving us levels
So everyone's roughly the same
If anyone turns out a bit different
They'll know which teacher to blame

I'm looking forward to football
And finishing off our display
And Miss says we'll go to a cheese farm
To make cheese and miss a whole day

Miss says that when it's all over
We'll do music and hand-printed hats
But today we must do as they say
Sit on our butts and do SATs

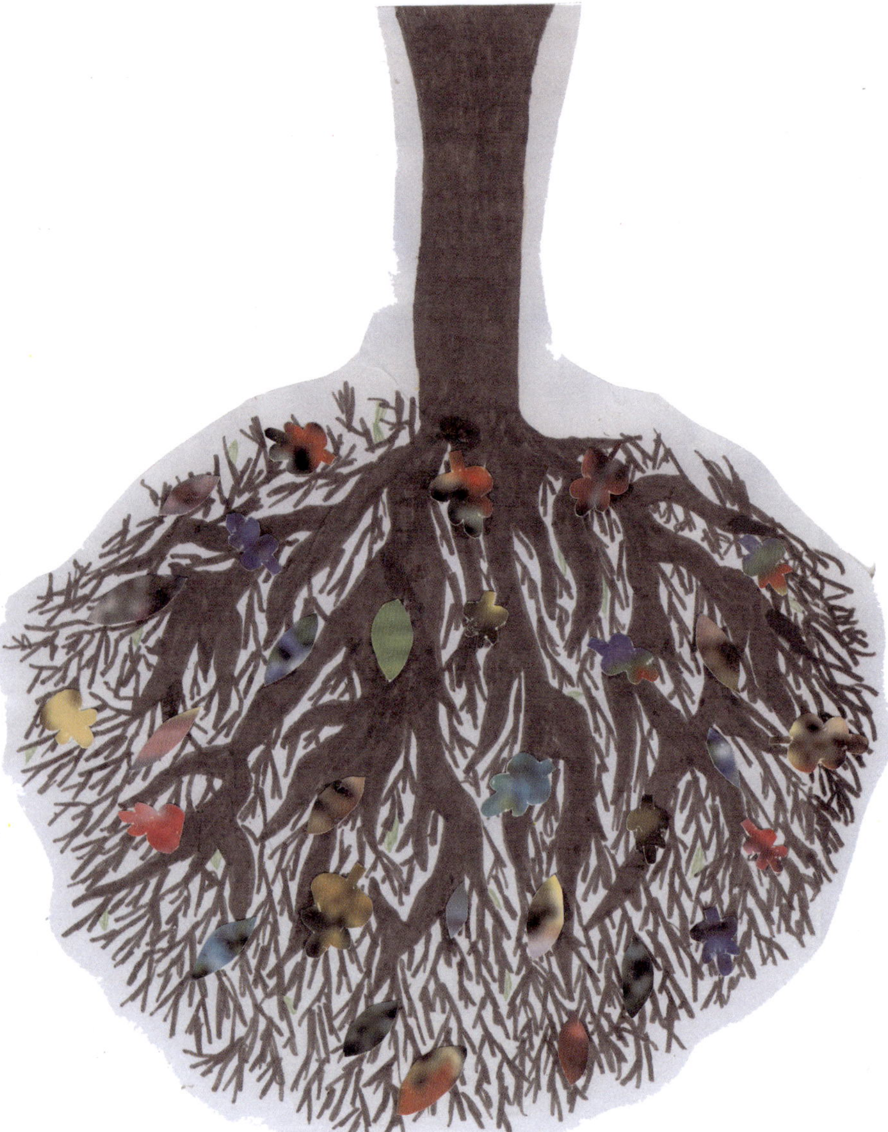

Trees

Before I woke
the old oak spoke:

Look after the trees

We breathe out
so you can breathe in

Our roots bind the earth
when it rains

We shade you
and give you fruit

We hold you up
when you climb

We stay after you are gone
We remember your stories

Proud Cat

... can't open the cat flap.
Its magnetic strip sometimes sticks.
She thinks it would be undignified
to hoist herself up and grip
or launch herself through and slip.
She likes to look cool, licking her whiskers.
She's nobody's fool.

'A cat on hot bricks? not me.
A cat in a fix? can't you see?
I'm taking my time. I'm fine.
Jumping through flaps or hoops
isn't my style. I have my pride.
If I was supposed to leap over things
I'd be a horse – of course'.

So my cat gets off my lap
ignores the flap and looks at me
with a heart-curdling soppy grin
and I have no choice
but to get up and let her out.
I'm thinking of having automatic
electric sliding doors put in.

Seal

My fat pads of oil-skinned flesh spread
over the rock like dough and glisten.
Blubber. Drip with a silver sheen but I'm so
heavy you wouldn't call it sleek.

Whiskers. Jowls. Damp nose like a dog's.
Eyes that are slits, then wide.
Wrinkles round my mouth like a comic aside.
No sharp edges. No sneer. Come near.

Come and see me slide over my rock,
tip in, splash, go under. See my bulk lift
and veer, corkscrew through the water,
pierce like a spear. Without a care. Here

I dance, I weave waves. Not just blues and greens
but red, brown, gold. I'm soap in their fingers.
I twist and turn. Know my own name.
Feel no shame.

Sloping back onto my rock with my flippers jutting out,
strange.
I am solid mass again, a bursting pod.
I slap myself down on the rock, hard

my hair coat brill-creamed, back-combed.
I could wise-crack, think of a joke.
Not this time. I lift my face up. Listen.
This is my voice. It calls up from the ocean bed,

a roar, a yelp full of silt, sea-water
and echoes in empty caves.
Can you hear me?
This is what I want to say.

Cricket

Batting like a demon
Bowling like a fox
Scoring like Harry Porridge
In his magic socks

Allergic to Spinach

I'm allergic to spinach
I can't eat cabbage or peas
Broccoli makes me feel funny
I go all weak at the knees

I come out in all sorts of nasties
When I swallow a single string bean
I've explained it to Mum – it's quite simple
I can't eat anything green

She tried hiding peas in the pasta
And disguising spinach as soup
And colouring leeks with ketchup
But no way would *I* be duped

I've told her over and over
She doesn't get what I mean
Not cabbage, not peas, not lettuce
I can't eat anything green

I'm allergic to spinach
I can't eat cabbage or sprouts
I'm sorry Mum it's official
Everything green is OUT!

Questions

When you ask me
How old is the moon?
What comes after space?
How do you know
if a snail is a boy?
What's that growling
down the plughole?
I realise how much finding out
I've still got to do

Goldilocks Says Sorry

it was me

came to visit when you weren't in
drank your lemonade mixed with gin

it was me

ate your strawberries ripe and red
left my swimming costume, wet, on your bed

it was me

used your phone to call Calcutta
smeared the handset with melted butter

it was me

played with your computer when I got bored
deleted all the files you had carefully stored

it was me

let your twin canaries go
flushed your goldfish down the toilet bowl

it was me

painted rainbows on your bedroom walls
stuffed your duvet with ping pong balls

it was me

read your diary, tried on your shoes
lay on your bed and had a snooze

it was me

woke and screamed at three pairs of eyes
didn't stop to apologise

it was me

upset your little one with deafening shouts
smashed your window jumping out

it was me

made up a story, I confess
sold my version to the tabloid press

it was me

talked about porridge and a broken chair
and a nasty encounter with some paranoid bears

it was me... it was me... sorry!

Ice Cream

Make some ice cream!
It's easier than it seems
with an ice cream machine.
You put in cream,

milk (unskimmed), maybe chocolate
or a biscuit – and whisk it –
switch the ON switch
with a flick of your wrist.

Twenty minutes
watch it churning
see it turning, turning colder
getting creamy in the bowl.

Be bold, be bolder!
Put in nuts, lemon, syrup
put in raisins, cocoa
let it fill up –

be daring – make your own concoction
never caring
what your Mum will say later when she sees it
you can freeze it –

or your Dad if he gets mad
it's the best fun you've had
such a cool feeling
never mind it's all over the ceiling!

Keep the switch on
ice cream all over the kitchen.
Tell your brother or your sister
this ice cream is miles better than a Twister.

Give them a taster
watch the expressions on their faces.
'How did you make it?'
'The recipe's a secret.'

'It's scrumptious – really fine –
better than ninety-nine Ninety Nines!'
Strawberry toffee minty coffee
what a mixture

revolving in your mouth
dissolving
make some ice cream
make some ice cream
                                    – go on!

Pen y Fan

'My best thing was climbing the hill' – Lily

Pen y Fan, Pen y Fan
climbing you is better than

cinnamon buns for breakfast
cushions all over the floor
the whispering and creaking
of the old oak door

Pen y Fan, Pen y Fan
climbing you is better than

crunch of feet on gravel
footsteps on the stairs
hiding in the priest-hole
if anybody dares

Pen y Fan, Pen y Fan
climbing you is better than

stars made of silver
a walk at night
voices round the fire
as flames flare bright

Pen y Fan, Pen y Fan
millions of years older than

all of us together
climbing high
you show us the sun
and the big blue sky

Animal Antics

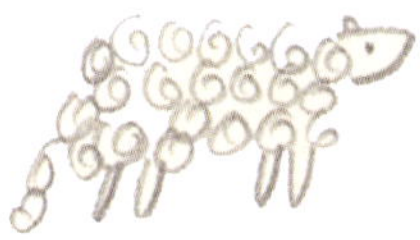

Thelma and Louise
hurtle across the field
baaing at the first sign of human.
They'd leap over the edge
if there wasn't a hedge.

Dolly wants to be in their gang –
she jumped the wire fence
in a woolly coat
strolled into a tent, stood on the mattress
and stared.

Rita Hayworth and Ginger Rogers
and sleek dark Grace Jones
cluck and peck, beaks down, bottoms up.
Ginger once pecked a boy's cut knee
thinking it was a slice of bacon.

Claude, Pip and Silvie play Who Can Be The Cutest?
Roll in the Grass, Sawdust Fights
Catch the Rope, Tease the Dog
Acrobatics on the Roof
Help I'm Stuck – Come and Rescue Me with a Blanket
(Not really!)

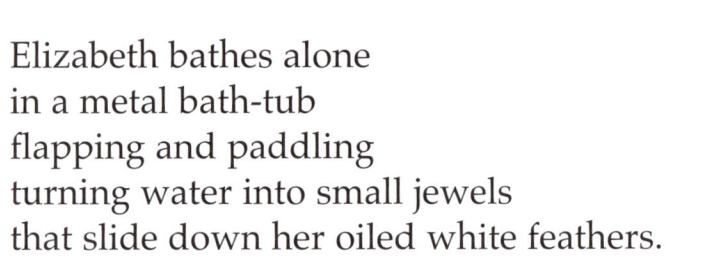

Elizabeth bathes alone
in a metal bath-tub
flapping and paddling
turning water into small jewels
that slide down her oiled white feathers.

Billie barks and lollops into the woods
muscles rippling under her brown fur
swims the river for sticks
flicks herself dry
With her total-body body-shake.

Snoopy sniffs the grass-sweet lanes
nose-twitching at every hint of blackberry,
acorn, hawthorn, rabbit, mouse,
breathing in a whole long
symphony of summer.

Valentine's Message

You're my oochy coochy coochy
You're my shuffle puffle woo
You're my inky pinky panky
My smoochy smoochy smoo

My tinky tonky too la
My ipsy wipsy way
My shilly shally shambles
My doo da doo da day

You're my Eureka, my overflowing bath
My fantastic discovery, my stunning aftermath
You're my perfect equation for total elation
My standing ovation, my overnight sensation

You're my colours of the rainbow, infra-red to indigo
You're the bit of gold that's gleaming on the end of Cupid's bow
You're my shining Everest, my fabulous K2
My Hotel Paradiso, my room with a view

I Love You

You're my Chelsea bun, my doughnut, my chocolate éclair
My picnic with the twiglets that we're going to share
You're my Guinness, my porridge, my dark Irish stew
You're the lightness in my laughter when I laugh with you

You're my funky rhythm, my gospel and my soul,
My longitude and latitude, my north and my south pole
You're my adjectives, my verbs, my future declension
You're lots of other things I've forgotten to mention

You're my oochy coochy coochy
You're my shuffle puffle woo
You're my inky pinky panky
My smoochy smoochy smoo

My tinky tonky too la
My ipsy wipsy way
My shilly shally shambles
My doo da doo da day

Summer

Go away grey clouds
It's summer time and it's June

It's warm and nearly the holidays
They've filled the paddling pool in the park

Out of the way grey clouds
Let us see the blue sky

Let us smell roses in front gardens
and paint our faces in street carnivals

Blow away grey clouds
it's warm and it's nearly the holidays

Go away grey clouds
It's summer time and it's June

Beach

We've made it. At last. Laid down our loads,
put up our flag, our confident, striped canvas banner,
staked out our territory, claimed our victory.

We trudged here through fifty weeks of alarm clocks,
half-drunk cups of coffee, missed buses, corridors,
eye-strain, aching feet, bills, phone calls, aspirations.

Now, everything is simple. Assured.
The sun is a bulging nectarine, the sea a rumpled bed.
Sand is particles of rock, the sky huge and always here.

We're going to make sandcastles, lick ice-creams,
rub oil into familiar shoulders.
We're going to forget. We're going to remember.

We're going to start again.

Silver Man

As I was walking on the sand
I met a strange and silver man
He asked me did I know the way
The way to the starry heaven

To him then did I reply
Oh silver man do tell me why
Why do you need to know the way
The way to the starry heaven?

As I was sailing on the sea
The silver man he came to me
He asked me did I know the way
The way to the deepest ocean

To him then did I reply
Oh silver man do tell me why
Why do you need to know the way
The way to the deepest ocean?

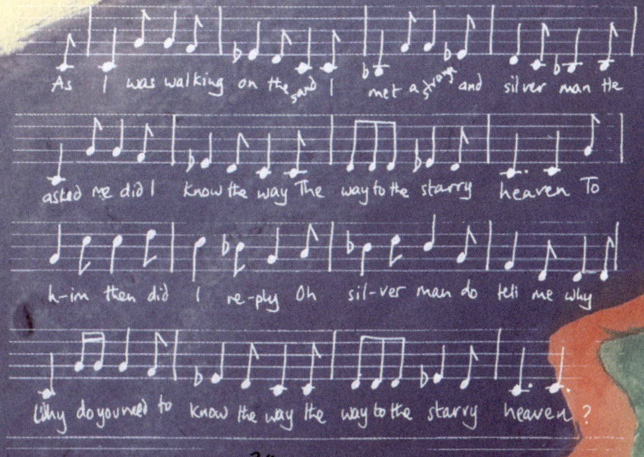

As I was climbing mountains high
The silver man came riding by
He asked me did I know the way
The way to the icy cavern

To him then did I reply
Oh silver man do tell me why
Why do you need to know the way
The way to the icy cavern?

And all at once I was alone
The silver man he had gone
I found there were many roads to home
The way that he did teach me

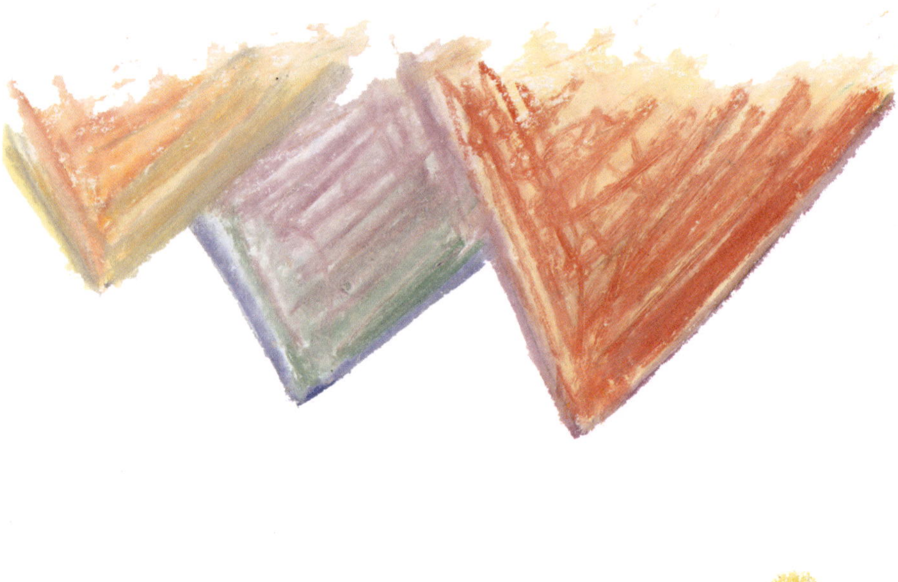

Egyptian Kaleidoscope

Four thousand years in musty rooms
Pyramids point to a blank-faced moon
Pharaohs fold arms in shadowed tombs
Lips closed tight in the hissing gloom

Above your deep and dreamless sleep
the silent stars go by

Hieroglyphic versions of secret charms
The mummified faces of kings embalmed
Animal gods protect them from harm
Watching over their locked-up karma

Above your deep and dreamless sleep
the silent stars go by

Enter the winter kaleidoscope turning
The starry night and the home fires burning
The cold north pole with bright snow falling
All across the world the sound of voices calling

Above your deep and dreamless sleep
the silent stars go by

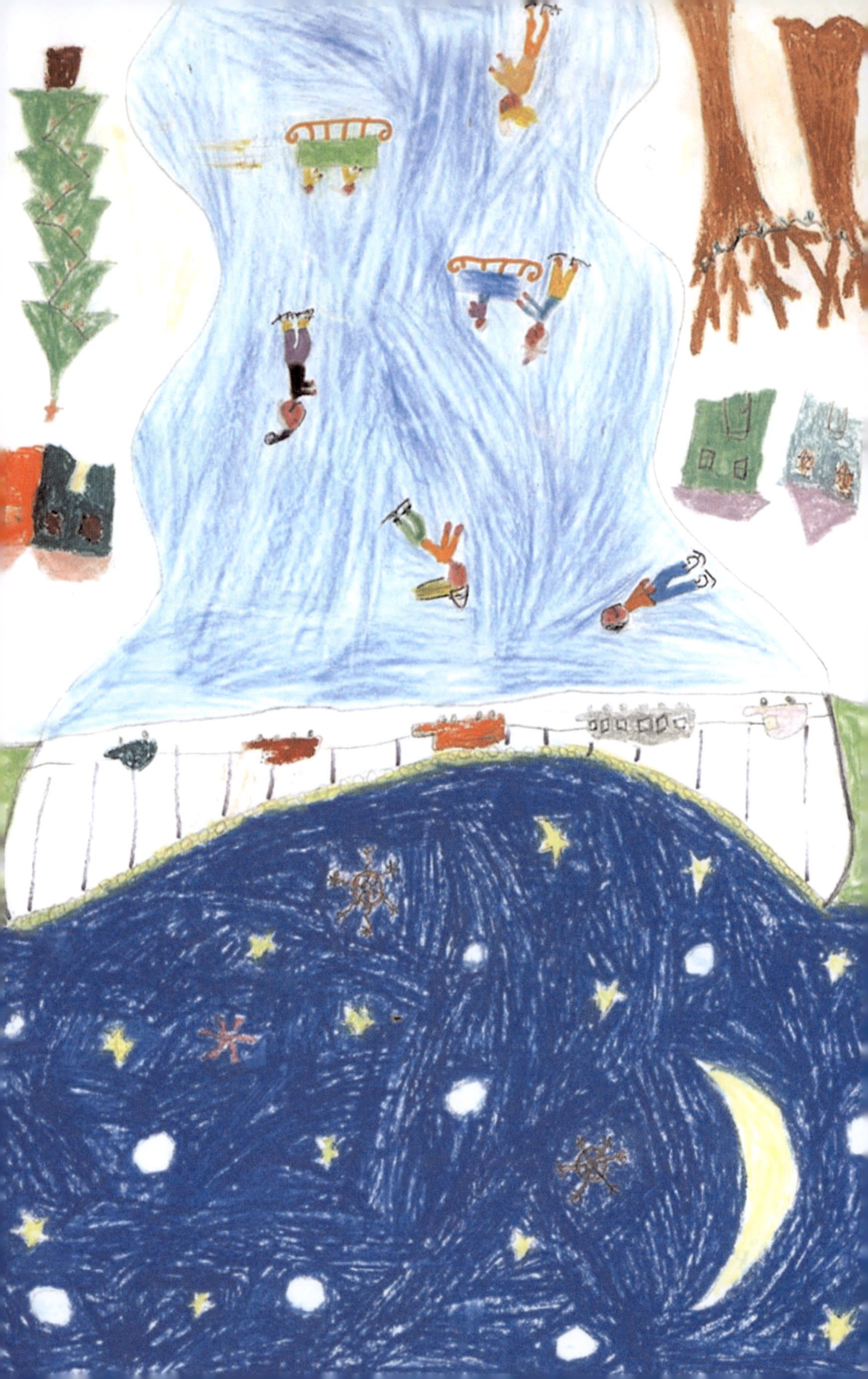

Skating

The moment's fleeting, fleeting
When you are skating
When you are skimming with your fleet feet
Over ice that is thin and may crack, interrupt
You may face the fact that
The moment's fleeting, fleeting

But oh the rush as you glide
Slide across smooth, fast
Fast through the air alive
Alive inside and so full of life
You could burst like a ripe grape
Oh the rush as you glide

This moment is holding
And in it you're fleeting
Your thin feet on pale ice skating
And all you can be is moving
Through cold air passing, breathing
Your warmth of being
Breathing your warm being

Celebration

A child is born
Wonderful
A child is born
Wonderful
A child is born
Wonderful
Let's celebrate with a song

A star shines bright
In the night sky
A star shines bright
In the night sky
A star shines bright
In the night sky
Let's celebrate with a song

These gifts are given
This winter time
These gifts are given
This winter time
These gifts are given
This winter time
Let's celebrate with a song

A Poet's Wish

I want to find a rhythm that you can't let go
I want to take words dancing, go fast, go slow

I want to share a secret, open a door
Show you places you haven't been before

I want to take you where it's out of bounds
Do some acrobatics with your adjectives and nouns

I want to weave you a story, spin you a yarn
Crack a joke and sound an alarm

I want to give you words for the worlds you see
So your poems grow like leaves on a tree

I want to sew words together and scatter them apart
I want to give you word-beats for the rhythms of your heart

Fiona Hamilton lives in Bristol, England.
In 2005 she won the Belmont Poetry Prize,
which is awarded to a poet whose work
proves most popular with children